STOP PLANNING AND START FINISHING

THE STORY OF AN AGILIST

SERGIO ZAMORA

y♥publico

STOP PLANNING AND START
FINISHING: THE STORY OF AN AGILIST
de Sergio E. Zamora Rubio

D. R. © Sergio E. Zamora Rubio
D. R. © Elvia Amalia Navarro Jurado
Juan de Dios Bátiz 29 B, 203, Lindavista
C.P. 07360 Gustavo A. Madero,
Ciudad de México, 2020.

Corrección de estilo: Oliver Davidson
Traducción: Giulia Magaña
Diseño editorial: Adriana Santiago
Primera edición: mayo 2023

First and foremost, I would like to thank my wife, Amalia Sandoval, for the support, inspiration, ideas and love she has given me throughout the writing of this little book. She still showers me with her love, and it motivates me to keep going. Thank you, my love. I want to thank my parents, Sergio and Luzma, who gave me not only life, nourishment, guidance and affection, but also the strength to move forward. By the way, that notebook is still blank.

Thank you, Carmen, Javier, Norma, Iván, Magali, Arturo, Rubén, Adriana, Ricardo, Joshua, Magda, and Juan; all of you were part of this adventure and gave me your support and guidance. My total respect goes to Gustavo, who has been not just a mentor, but more importantly a friend who inspired me to go above and beyond.

Thank you, Mym and Fer, for convincing me this was possible. Thank you, Héctor Ortega, for all the advice and support you gave me in order to write this work.

And thank you for taking the time to read this. I wish you the very best of journeys!

Prologue

There'll always be serendipity involved in discovery.
—Jeff Bezos

After a number of years working as a programmer, I became interested in project management, especially software—related projects. At the same time, I realized that the software that I was developing was not an end but a means towards something better, something we programmers did not know about. At that moment, I became interested in other business units within companies. Attempting to understand the business world, I came to the conclusion that the way to link both realms (software and business) was through project management. And thus I began to learn about it.

Agility was a wonderful discovery once I realized project management was largely based on administering the triple constraint of scope, time and budget. On the other hand, I well noticed that there was very little analysis around the business results.

Nowadays, after years of experience, I am interested on improving the flow of teams developing digital products by fostering suitable environments for learning, looking out for the wellbeing of people and focusing on the opportunities and the impact that digital products can deliver to clients.

This has not been easy an journey, but it has been fun (at least most of it). More importantly, it has allowed me to meet a great deal of people.

In 2016, I had the wonderful chance to integrate agility into a leading company within Mexico's financial sector. One of my tasks was forming a team of agility agents that would build the concept into every corner of the organization. I had recently arrived at Mexico and lacked a robust contact network to find the people and talent I needed. I wanted to find agents with the necessary drive for the job, so I began showing up at small forums about agility.

At one point, a young man (our author) caught my eye. He talked about Kanban and agility very differently from the other speakers. His examples were clear, yet impactful. I could tell he was there to share something, and not because he needed to stroke his ego or because he was looking for an opportunity to sell himself as an agility "expert". He discussed everything in a very natural way and had no intention of appearing like a guru, but most of all, he was not afraid of showing what he had learned from experiences that could be perceived as "failures".

My experience told me he could be a key element in bringing about transformation within my organization. After these many years, I can say I was right .

Nowadays, I enjoy the stories he captured in this book with a clear language and his characteristic way of narrating his experiences: with simplicity and no intention of appearing as an expert, but with the humility of someone who knows life is a constant journey where there is much to learn. And sharing that knowledge can help others, which is very satisfying.

I discovered the talent I needed, but by mere chance I found a friend (serendipity).

Gustavo Bonalde

BANI attacks us!

We can choose courage or we can choose comfort,
but we can't have both. Not at the same time.
—Brené Brown

I dare say that 90% of our actions depend on the tools derived from software development. This causes information to move at great speeds: all processes, projects, initiatives, and relationships have suffered radical changes and are now much more dynamic. The term BANI has recently come up. It is an acronym for Brittle, Anxious, Nonlinear and Incomprehensible, all of them adjectives that define the ever—changing environment in which we live. Still, despite the sheer amount of information, it makes it cumbersome to easily adapt to rapid changes and overcoming or understanding uncertainty.

This affects us not only as individuals: companies are struggling as well since traditional management has become obsolete. The issue is not exclusive to the technology industry, but rather involves small or medium—sized companies looking to provide any sort of customer service, and this is due to clients raising the standards of satisfaction.

Think about how easy it is nowadays to get a taxi or book a flight. Now think about any kind of service and I can guarantee that there is at least one app that can offer it. Downloading and using it is simple, just as simple as deleting it if you are dissatisfied with the service. **In the 21st century, clients can get rid of your services simply with a swipe on their phone.** And for these reasons, we need to change the way that we think, work and learn. To achieve that, many of us have decided on the road and values that the Agile Manifesto offers us.

In the past twenty years, the word "agile" has had a lot of impact on software developers and other professionals. It is safe to say that these values have been adapted and used by other departments beyond software with the intent of conquering today's problems, overcoming that BANI environment, increasing our resilience, surviving and thriving.

We "agilists" aim to understand our environment, get to know the system within which we develop and learn from the constant stream of experiences so that we may adapt and improve it. And not only that. We want to share that knowledge, so we can help each other grow and thrive. Our goal is to live each day with the values of agility. We want to collaborate with those around us, not just professionally, but on a personal level as well. We want to improve constantly, face challenges to learn and fulfill our purpose. We wish to contribute something valuable every day, whether that is an activity or just a phrase that fosters improvement. And last but not least, we reflect on our actions daily, and we ask ourselves if these are in line with our way of thinking.

In my opinion, one does not become an agilist in a two—day certification course, but it does not take a million years either. We may find ourselves in a comfort zone, grinding away, without seeking changes or challenges. I am not saying that there is anything wrong with this, but a significant part of being an agilist is constant improvement.

The heart of agility is in the passion that agilists show in displaying their values and principles daily. Don't take this the wrong way. I will explain myself paraphrasing Anton Ego in *Ratatouille:* "Not everyone can become a great agilist, but a great agilist can come from anywhere".

17

Becoming a great agilist is not an impossible task, but a journey with highs and lows, like any other journey. And just like any other journey, it begins somewhere. Let me tell you about the time I almost succeeded in becoming an agilist within a big company.

Following in my father's footsteps

Times are bad. Children no longer obey their
parents and everyone is writing a book.
—Cicero

A few years ago, I was an external consultant for a Huge
Company. I did technical analysis and coded a bit in SQL.
Due to my experience and the time within the company, I
was taking on the duties of a "technical leader", which, as

I see it, just means adding management of a team. Yes, you have more responsibilities and it helps your career grow, but since I did not actually have the position, I had to perform as a system's analyst and team leader, all while getting paid the same. And so a few years went by. I even became accustomed and comfortable. Then, after some time, thanks to my good performance, they offered me an actual position within the company.

I asked for some time to think about it. My father had worked twenty years for Huge Company, which made the decision very difficult. I had always said to myself I would not work there given how stressful my father's professional life had been. I did not have any intention of working at a place where you check in, but you do not check out, weekends belong to the boss, and don't get me started on what that can do to your health. **From my point of view, there is no connection between working more hours and being more successful.**

When I think about it, I can tell you that change is not simple. At the time, I wanted to buy a house to live with my girlfriend. We had been together some years now, and I was sure she was the one. I wanted to take that important step. I wanted to be financially stable. I wanted to get married. And at the same time, I wanted to work at a nice place where I could grow and develop my skills. I have always tried to learn and practice those lessons. I consider myself driven to challenges, as long as they are interesting and in line with my personal goals. I knew that if I stayed as a consultant, it would take me longer to get a raise; also, I had no idea if anybody took my job as a technical leader seriously, and there was a good chance I might find myself filling these two roles for years to come.

"This could be a great opportunity", I thought to myself. Huge Company is an international brand with many years of history. Working at a place with such a big market presence looks great on your resume. As for my father's negative experience, I was sure they would have changed their work culture by then. So, I took the offer.

Just because you can't see the issue, that doesn't mean it's gone

A journey of a million miles begins with a single step.
—Lao Tse

Years went by and I kept working for Huge Company, during which time there were many changes. It had become one of those "Best Place to Work" kind of companies, so not everything was bad. Unless you are one of those people who cannot keep your mouth shut when you see something wrong. For example, I was the "technical leader" of three projects, and boy was I overworked.

One of the problems I had was that, apparently, my job was invisible. Thanks to digitalization, everything is generated through tickets, emails and chats. It is easy to lose track of all the things you have to do. However, projects at Huge Company were different and they were reviewed in a monthly meeting where all the technical leaders reported on their progress. Strangely enough, we all showed progress of a 99% rate or in green (I have no idea why green is an indicator that everything is going hunky—dory). The thing is, I knew how to ~~cheat~~ show my progress. But I actually had no idea how my coworkers were doing. From time to time, I would summon the courage and show a yellow number. This would get me two reactions:

1. Get yelled at for doing a crummy job and having poor time management.
2. Grudgingly ask for help, since everyone was pretty busy and actually helping meant more work.

Out of my three projects, one showed good progress. The second one was so big that, to be honest, I only got involved when I had time to spare. The third was a bit behind because of some security issues (and I was sure it would be delayed). I began noticing this situation was constant for everybody. People can feel overwhelmed, and at times

24

asking for help or pointing out a problem makes you look incompetent or simply not cut out for your job.

But there is something wrong with a work environment where asking for help is seen as a sign of incompetence.

On the other hand, collaboration was scarce. Everyone showed the progress of their own projects. And while we gave each other a hand, getting yelled at or being praised happened at a personal level. Leaders that had more projects were viewed more favorably, regardless of their status: they made it seem like they were worth their salt, unlike those leaders who only had one or two projects.

25

I remember once a project went into production and crashed. We stayed up until very late to solve the bugs, some of us had to work during the weekend. Ultimately, the problem was solved. We were applauded for our commitment and our sense of urgency. Next month we made an update and since we had learned from our mistakes, it went great. No bugs. No one congratulated us for a job well done.

I was confused. How come when you mess up at work, but then you fix it on overtime, you get praised, but when you do it well from the get go, no one cares? Anyway, problems seemed to never end. They had become an everyday thing. Excessive work was normal, just as the lack of collaboration and the silos between departments. But that's just work in IT, right? We are the geeks, the freaks that put on a pair of headphones, lock the doors and code away.

I'd rather not go

What you deny subdues you. What you accept transforms you.
—Carl Gustav Jung

One day, I arrived at the offices of Huge Company. It was a day like any other, except on that particular morning we had an urgent meeting. We did not have a lot of context about it. All I knew was that urgent meetings only result in more work and/or being scolded.

The head of the department was there, whom for the purposes of this text we will call "Chief". A friend of mine, the manager of a different department who we will call "Daysi", was also there. And finally, my brand manager, Seb.

The Chief had received an invitation from the senior management to send agents for training outside of Mexico about a new tool. Not long before I had told Daysi that I wanted to do something different. I needed a challenge and I asked for her help. I was tired of undertaking projects that had no specific goal, the only purpose of which seemed mindless work. I was fed up that every single suggestion for change I came up with was being ignored. I was tired of getting the same answer after proposing a different way to do things: "This is how we do it." But the most frustrating was that I did what I was asked, and somehow it was not enough. I had no professional development. I had not taken any type of training or course. And economically, they had only raised my salary in accordance with what the law required. This was a considerable limitation on my dreams of buying a house, getting married and moving in with my girlfriend. However, people say you should be careful with what you wish for because you might just get it.

The purpose of the meeting was to decide who would take that training, and Daysi had remembered our conversation. She brought up my name, but since I was not working for Daysi, we needed Seb's approval. He said: "If he feels like it, fine. As long as he does not drop the three projects he has." That meant to me one thing: more work.

I asked what was the purpose of the training and if I would use that tool in my projects. The Chief needed people who knew about databases so they could learn how to use the tool, apply it in projects, and train others on how to use it. Again, all I could think was "more work".

Five words came out of my mouth: "Can I think about it?" The Chief, Seb and Daysi looked at each other and then at me. "I need to send the names of the people who are going, so we need to know your answer right now", said the Chief. At that moment, I believed this training would not benefit me at all, but rather increase my workload, so I gave what I thought was the most sensible answer. I clenched my teeth, swallowed and said: "No, thank you."

Given the frustration I was enduring, my thoughts were very negative. Having an insane amount of work that you cannot visualize or frame can take you down the terrible road of multitasking. Being overwhelmed and unmotivated led me to choose my current situation. The famous comfort zone.

The Chief said: "Alright, as you wish."

I left the room feeling annoyed, but at the same time, happy. I was brave enough to say no. I believed I had refrained from multitasking. I had read that, on a personal level, multitasking makes you 40% less productive and causes a 50% increase of the time it takes to get the job done compared to being focused. **If you concentrate on staying focused, you will avoid wasting time in multitasking. Yes. I had done it.**

I was on my way to my desk, but before I could to sit down, Daysi smacked the back of my head.

"Why did you reject the offer?", she asked. "You've been telling me you want to do things differently, take on new challenges. This is your chance. This is why I dropped your name."

I explained the rationale for my answer. "I don't want to have to do more things that I'm already doing. If I go to the training, I'll be overloaded and start failing. I'll end up turning things late, and then I'll be scolded."

Daysi has always been a good friend, and without intending it, a great mentor. She explained every important change demands an effort and in most cases, more time spent working. The great advantage is that if those changes are part of our goals and ambitions, we understand that there is a long—term benefit and it is easier to devote that extra time and effort.

"If you don't change your mind, you will stay here waiting for the perfect opportunity, and the odds are it won't happen. Worst of all, you are probably going to regret not taking this chance".

Daysi's words echoed in my head. I saw the whole thing in a different light. I was being offered a fully paid trip overseas to get training. True, I would have to login and work extra hours, but this would be something new. An opportunity to learn.

I shoved Daysi aside and darted towards the Chief's office. "I'll go!" I yelled.

"Do you have a passport and visa?"

I froze. I had not left Mexico in a while. All I could do was tell him I would check. The Chief gave me until the end of the day to look it up. I immediately called home. They looked at the documents. The passport was still valid. OK, one down. Unfortunately, my visa had expired. I informed the Chief I had to renew it. He made it very clear I had only one week to do so, otherwise I would not go.

That very instant, I called to ask what I had to do. It was a bureaucratic labyrinth! They explained that since it had expired less than three months ago, I could get an appointment without an interview, but that it would take two weeks. That was not an option. I explained this was a business trip. They told me that they could expedite the process if I had a letter from the company requesting so. Furthermore, if they printed the visa directly on the passport instead of a card, it would be even faster.

It made me think that, as a client, you always want your request to be resolved as fast as possible. However, there are processes, capacity and most of all, requests that are not urgent. In order for the embassy to treat my request as urgent, it had to meet certain requirements; otherwise, I would have to go through the normal process. It would be great if we could replicate this in organizations or in government institutions and simply sending an email a request could escalate the level of urgency. There should be policies and explicit agreements to classify something as urgent.

The embassy had it pretty clear, so I went to the Chief and asked for the letter. That same afternoon I went to the embassy and I dropped my passport and the letter. My visa would be ready in three days. I immediately called the Chief. "Okay, I will add your name, but only as a possible candidate until you get your visa. Once you do, book your flight and get any other paperwork done."

Three days went by. During this time, I spoke to Daisy about the trip, and she gave me advice. She and Jaime, another good friend, had gone several times, so they gave me a full schedule, places for dining and sightseeing. In my opinion, Jaime was the best solutions architect Huge Company had. He always shared his knowledge with me, and he was always there to help me whenever I asked. He recommended I study a bit and prepare some questions.

"Even if you are going for a training, you should be prepared. That shows interest and professionalism."

At that moment, I was glad to have friends and people I could trust at work. **Interpersonal relationships need to be fostered: they help communication flow more effectively, increase motivation and strengthen collaboration.**

Do you have friends at your current job? Is there somebody you admire? I hope the answer to at least one of these questions is yes. If not, you should take a good look around your workplace.

At long last, the visa arrived, and the Chief sent the confirmation. Everything was ready. I was very excited. It was all going according to plan and nothing could stop me. That day, at the airport, Seb sent me an email in which he copied the Chief. It was a list of work I had to get done and a plan to follow during my absence.

Prepare for turbulence

Anger, pride, and competition are our real enemies.
—Dalai Lama

It was the worst flight of my life. The word "turbulence" elevated to a whole new meaning. This was turbulence within. Among the activities I was expected to complete while I was gone, some I simply could not understand: "Must ensure 100% availability whenever necessary".

What on Earth did that mean!? Was I supposed to sit through the training and oversee my team at the same time?

"There must be no delays in the work plan herein attached." In the two weeks of training, I was supposed to turn in some progress around my three projects, including the one that needed approval from security. How was I supposed to deliver something the other departments had not authorized yet? And finally, the most ridiculous part: "Send a daily report of your activities." I was angry. I was stressed. I was sad. "Told you so" said the little voice in my head.

I understand companies wanting to maximize the time their employees have at hand to boost results, but precisely this type of management is obsolete for a knowledge economy. Today's work requires creativity, focus, and many changes. **More working hours do not increase creativity. It is necessary to have space to think and reflect.** Not to mention that I had been sent to take a training where my ability to learn would be seriously impaired if I was not fully involved. **If companies invest their money on training, why can't they invest in giving people enough time to learn** instead of constantly interrupting them because they think this is some sort of vacation? In reality, they are wasting resources: at the end of the day, people do not learn what they were supposed to, and neither can they work since their focus is elsewhere. The thing that stressed me the most was that the plane was about to take off. I was writing an email in response when a flight attendant asked me to turn off my electronic devices, so I did.

My head was still reeling when the plane took off. I came up with a metaphor of the plane taking off and my dreams of learning calmly getting smaller and smaller. Ángel, a coworker with a long career at Huge Company, was on the flight with me. I cannot imagine how I looked like during the flight, but he turned to me: "I don't mean to be nosy, but is everything okay? You seem tense."

Usually I would have answered that everything was fine, or that the flight made me nervous, or something subtle to get him to leave me alone. This time I felt so anxious that I thought "What's the worst that can happen?"

I told him about the email and how it made me feel and how badly I wanted to jump ship. Ángel's answer was simple and powerful: "What's the benefit if your reply is a dismissal?"

I thought about it for a second, and all I could answer was that I would blow some steam. Ángel then told me that since I was leaving for a course, Seb probably felt pressured as well, and that resulted in this anxiety—driven email. We cannot control other people's reactions, but we can control our own.

"If you answer angry, frustrated and with every intention of venting, you'll repeat the pattern, and you'll mirror that anger. You'll only grow the discontent without solving anything. Instead, think about something more productive before we land."

And so I went through the actions that were within reach, who I could lean on in my team for complicated tasks that required more people, as well as possible solutions for things beyond me.

As I reflected on these things, the email that had felt like the end of my life as a free man started to seem less and less important. Once I arrived at my destination, I grabbed my laptop and answered exactly how Ángel had advised me to. I itemized what I would do and explained why it was inefficient to send a daily report on my activities.

I asked for help from my team members to avoid delays in the current plan and delegated activities, provided their workload allowed for it. I finished the email by stating that I would be available as long as it did not interfere with the training, that I would prioritize it, and I would go back to my assignments during breaks or after the sessions.

I felt a little calmer. I had provided an intelligent response to visceral matter. I did not get a reply to my message, probably because the response was unexpected. Since I was not playing along and did not display any sort of anger, the situation was diffused. I realized that it is much better to be level—headed when facing these types of situations, rather than raging on. This is a good reason to work on your emotional intelligence. Had it not been for Ángel, I have no idea what would have been my answer.

Now I could close my laptop and call my family to let them know I had arrived well. Feeling hungry, I headed to the hotel's restaurant and found Ángel having dinner. I joined him and told him about my email.

"That's a good answer. Smart and collected."

I thanked him for his advice, but felt embarrassed we had not talked before at the office, so I told him.

Ángel understood that sometimes work is so overwhelming we become fully devoted to it, but we should also look around and engage with each other. Most likely, somebody else has already gone through that seemingly impossible problem. That was Ángel's great advantage. His twenty years working for Huge Company made his experience very valuable. But at the same time, I felt uneasy about companies setting aside expert people who are willing to share their knowledge. These are leaders without an official position, and I was happy I had found one.

All good, thanks for asking

When the student is ready, the teacher will appear.
—Zen proverb

I woke up early so I could at least get a half–an–hour run. I went down for breakfast with my suitcase and found Ángel sipping on his coffee. After we finished, our commute was a 30–minute drive to the office. I was unaware Huge Company owned facilities such as the learning center we were in, and was happy to know that they had this infra-structure and cared about their employees. There was a room for us with movable chairs so we could collaborate; at the back there were cookies, coffee, water, and fruit.

The instructor arrived a few minutes later. He welcomed us and asked to wait for everyone else, then gave us nametags. The instructor walked up to the board and put post—its on one side of it. Then he drew columns. Above the post—its he wrote "Learning subject". The first column was titled "Learn-ing", the second one said "Check learning" and the third was "Completed". I found it interesting, it looked like a planner.

There were flip boards around the room with differ-ent texts, values, principles and agreements. Also, one had written "Parking lot" on it. I began to think that we were at the wrong room, so I checked the door. Indeed this was the designated room. I was even more confused. I walked back inside and asked the instructor if this was the training room for the new database tool. He smiled and said yes.

More people arrived, some from other countries. Now the training could get started. It was really weird, I had never had such a "humane" learning session. We had to make agreements at the beginning of the session, such as behaviors and stating our expectations. The courses I had been to were more like: "Here's the coursebook, check the slides. Repeat. Repeat. Repeat." But in this case there was a lot of interaction between us, with discussions and values. I wondered about the tool.

During a break, I asked the instructor about it, and he told me that in order to use the tool, we first had to consider the work scenarios in which we might want to use it. After we went through each subject, we had a session of agreements and wrapped it up.

After the introductions, expectations and agreements, we got to a post—it that said "Agile Manifesto". That training, that session, that very moment was my first approach to the Agile Manifesto, and it is still present in my life. It made me understand there are multiple ways into software development.

The first phrase of the manifesto blew my mind:

We are uncovering better ways of developing software by doing it and helping others do it.

At long last, we were talking about finding better ways! If anything had me frustrated at Huge Company, it was going through the same management. The same steps. The same documents. The same processes. The same rules.

We can all agree that new problems have emerged in the past ten years. Why should we develop software in the same old way? Also, the word "helping" brought me a lot of hope: we could share our experiences and help each other. Experience and collaboration are some of the few assets that only really exist when shared. I had just met Ángel, and he helped me with something so simple and yet so complex as answering an email. I felt excited knowing I could learn from other people.

Something that greatly enriches agility is diversity. That is why we need to promote the idea that help and wisdom can come from anywhere. But things kept getting better: this first phrase was followed by the values that guide agilists:

> **Individuals and interactions** *over processes and tools*
> **Working software** *over comprehensive documentation*
> **Customer collaboration** *over contract negotiation*
> **Responding to change** *over following a plan*
> *That is, while there is value in the items on the right, we value the items on the left more.*

I was awe–struck. The more I read it, the more I liked it. Thinking about people and acknowledging that our interactions are more valuable than processes or tools made me reconsider the projects I lead. I even wondered why we went to a training about a tool. We learn more from a conversation than from writing an email.

The instructor took the opportunity to comment on this. The reason they were telling us about agility first was because this tool was only as good as how you use it. If the tool would only prompt more processes, less interaction, and less collaboration, then the tool itself is not bad: rather, we are misusing it.

That is why the first part of the training had to do with changing our mindset, or at least opening our minds a little, in order to change the way we would work with the tool. Agility requires a "believe it to see it" mentality, since in order to see the changes, we have to first believe in their value. I will not get into detail about the Agile Manifesto, [1] but I can tell you that at that moment it was a war cry to me. A statement of principles that laid bare that we were sick and tired of bad projects. Of selfish superheroes that would not share their knowledge. Of plans that praised you by how well you followed instructions and forgot about the end goal. After many years of feeling like another cog in the machine, I began to see that we could be individuals within a community.

At the end of the first day, we went for dinner and talked about what we had learned. I wanted to discuss so many things I had learned. I even told Daysi and Jaime about my first day. I sent them a link to the Manifesto, and we talked about it, mostly the part about documentation. I had forgotten the last time a training got me so excited. It felt great, so much so, answering emails regarding my other projects did not feel like a chore. I did it in the best way possible, and with a lot of motivation. Yes, feeling motivated gave me a different perspective, even though there were many challenges ahead. I knew I was "uncovering better ways of developing software by doing it and helping others do it".

---

1   https://agilemanifesto.org/lso/en/manifesto.html

As the training progressed, we dealt into the framework. We saw a bit of Scrum, the famous framework that a lot of people claim to know, but not many practice. I will not go into details about Scrum either since there are numerous online resources available.[2] In my experience, it is one of the books we least refer to in order to understand Scrum.

Personally, the part that stays with me is the values:

Courage

Focus

Commitment

Respect

Openness

It is a light framework to develop and maintain complex products. The conversation focused on roles and events, but the instructors explained that this is just one of the many ways of fostering agility and that before jumping into conclusions, we should listen and pay attention in the following days.

There was a section called Parking Lot where we could leave questions that would be answered later on that day, or if we were out of time, at the end of the course. I asked if all events were really necessary. All I could think about was these daily 15–minute meetings and how disastrous

---

2   https://scrumguides.org/index.html

they could be on my team. The day ended with us cutting up magazines and building a mockup app with those clippings.

I understood how important it was to have a facilitator by your side. One thing that was wrong about my projects was that we had a list of requirements, but feedback was nonexistent. We were only waiting for the next stage to begin so we could make changes to the requirements we had misunderstood, or that we developed hastily just to comply with the due date.

For me, the most exciting day was when we studied Kanban. At the beginning, it was a little confusing because they called it the Kanban Method, and from what I understood, there were no methodologies within Agile. I think the Kanban guide[3] explains this better.

Kanban is frequently mistaken with a methodology or a framework. In software engineering, a methodology is an approximation to the definition of software development processes and project management (a somewhat inadequate name for "methodology", which means "the study of methods"). Methodologies contain work flows and defined prescriptive processes, including roles and responsibilities. This means that, generally, they are specific to a certain domain, like software development. On the other hand, a framework is an incomplete methodology: it is a series of

---

3   https://resources.kanban.university/kanban—guide/

structures destined to a more general application, but it needs to be customized to adapt to a specific context.

But Kanban is not a methodology or a framework. It is a management method that can be applied to an existing process or way of work. The advantage is it can be incorporated into any process to improve it: it is an alternative path to agility.

To learn this method, its values (which I detailed in my blog years later[4]), practices and principles, we used a simulation.

For the first time, I was able to see that there are different ways to do things. Not everything depended on my project managers or on the traditional management approach I had used for almost ten years now. **You do not have to rely on the newest or the most used management method, but rather the one that helps you meet your goals.**

This trip had really been worth it, even the late nights working. I was motivated to take these strategies and apply them in my day to day. I also learned the value of training within an organization, of educating and reskilling the employees. These is very important, but most of all, it is inspiring. The first week was coming to an end, and that Friday they discussed a role that gave me a great deal of excitement: agile coaches.

---

4   https://fullmetalagilist.wordpress.com

The phrase "thank god it's Friday!" has always been confusing. It would seem that if you look forward so anxiously for the weekend, it must be because your job makes you unhappy. I think this can change from week to week. There were times I really anticipated the weekend, but there were others I did not want the week to end. In my opinion, it depends on the situation. Life is a box of chocolates, I suppose.

That Friday started off a bit weird. There were three strangers in the room. I liked them from the very beginning because they brought coffee and doughnuts with them (yes, giving sugar to the team is always motivating). The instructor introduced them as the agile coaches. "Oh, man. Are we getting coaches? Am I getting a workout? Do they know psychology?" Using the Lyssa Adkins model,[5] they explained that an agile coach guides you in your journey through agility by giving you the perspective of a mentor, a coach, an agility practitioner, a facilitator with a technical and business–oriented expertise.

When I heard that, I thought of Daysi and Jaime: both had been my coaches without having the actual position. The three strangers introduced themselves. I will call the third one BeeGee, a Kanban specialist. At the end of the day, we shared our expectations with agility, whether they

---

5   https://agilecoachinginstitute.com/agile—coaching—re-
    sources

made sense to us, and if it was possible to put some of this into practice. I felt in a safe environment, which is very important for there to be trust. I told them about some of the issues I noticed in my department, and they asked for details. Then they helped me see where I could have some influence, where I needed to ask for help, and what was beyond my reach. It was enriching to have an outside perspective that, through this tool, showed me how to solve my problems.

We agreed on an early wrap–up and celebrate the end of the theory section. You still remember we were going to learn about a tool, right? We went for dinner, ate a lot, and I went back to the hotel to send the report I had been asked to write. It was a short: "Everything is going smoothly thanks to our great team. Have a good weekend." One thing I had learned was to build trust within the team and let them know I would support them should anything go wrong.

It was a relaxing weekend. While Ángel and other people from the training went for a barbecue, I decided to go my own way. I rented a bike and went off exploring; I reflected on how complicated it is to ride a bike. You must keep your balance and rhythm, have confidence and be steady. Any small change can make you stumble and fall. The saying goes that once you learn something, you never forget it. It must be similar to the way we learn and work. How deeply some practices we find normal get ingrained in our mind, and out of habit or mere laziness, we never challenge them?

50

Staying in our comfort zone is simple. I like biking because it allows me to experience a place from a different perspective. You can explore it from the less expected corners. Unlike a car, where you only get down once you arrive at your destination, biking also lets you enjoy the journey. That was precisely what I was doing in this training: enjoying the learning experience. Even while the most difficult part was nearing and I would have to put everything into practice.

At the beginning of the new week, we were explained how the tool worked. It was not a big deal, it was just an interface to query a database visually and through objects. The interesting part was how the search queries and the objects were generated. The team that invited us to the training was responsible for the tool: it was their product. Part of the process was inviting more "clients" so they could use it and give them feedback and request changes and features. While they showcased the tool, we would ask questions or make requests, and they developed them in real time. They showed us how to solve the issue and we would decide whether we understood and then move on with the activity.

As end users, we were sitting next to the developers and gave them unfettered feedback. At the same time, two other people would capture our requests in another tool, took notes and oversaw the development process. This tool was a digital board where every request was a ticket we raised. The team worked it over, and as they did, we would try another feature or just watch while they worked on our requests. Once it was done, we were taught how to use the new features and then we validated them with preloaded data.

Our productivity was impressive. We would make three to five changes or requests daily, which ranged from giving the users an avatar to rounding up any figures displayed. Having an end user sitting next to the developers, someone teaching you how to use the product and someone else developing the documentation and tracking, it was a thing of beauty!

At the end of the second week, we ran a test with information from our own databases. It worked perfectly. But that was not the end of it. They gave us two simple tasks: show the tool to more information owners, train them, and if any changes were needed, request them through tickets; and using agility and the work process, values and principles we had learned.

Ironically, the former seemed complicated and the latter was the easy part, but I was so wrong!

That Friday, we went for dinner to say our goodbyes. I took the opportunity to tell BeeGee I was interested in learning more about Kanban, and he asked me to email him. He said he would send me the information and even mentor me.

I was excited. I felt like I was not alone: someone with experience and knowledge was on my side and ready to support me.

Obligation or responsibility?

With great power comes great responsibility.
—The Amazing Spider—Man

I was incredibly excited on our flight back. The trip had been worthwhile and I had learned a lot, but I kept thinking about the task we had been assigned: to use and share agility, its way of working, the values and principles that we had learned. One of my weaknesses is that I overthink things and worry too much. This situation made me think if we would actually be able to use agility at Huge Company. We had many things against us: only Ángel and I had taken this training, and while I might count on Daysi and Jaime, we were few. I was not even sure whether the Chief would be willing to adopt not only the way of working, but also the way of thinking.

I was getting stressed and wondered what I had gotten myself into. But at the same time, I remembered the beginning of the Agile Manifesto: "We are uncovering better ways..." But better ways for whom? For me? For Huge Company? I had to figure out how my work goals aligned with my personal goals.

Before this trip, I had the feeling of living and working in a loop. The frustration of not being recognized for my work choked me and made me feel belittled, trapped in my position because it was difficult to ask for a raise or a promotion. I remembered what I looked for in the short and long term: buying a house, living with my girlfriend, getting married, financial stability, working at a good company, growing and developing my skills. My expectations were high; having worked at Huge Company for several years, I did not see them materializing or at least approaching. To be honest, my lack of passion for my work showed in bitter comments. **A bad work environment can turn the best collaborator into the worst of all.**

This journey, this training, this intention to work with the agile values and principles were an opportunity to make changes. But were they all my responsibility?

Christopher Avery described the mental process of taking responsibility over an issue. [6] He states that we own the ability and power to create, choose and attract. In this case, it was up to me whether to share and use agility at Huge Company. It is natural that at first, the answer is negative due to fear, habit or lack of interest. But my goals encouraged me to act differently. I must understand the value of my actions. This also helps me to promote and make my work more visible. I can blame others for being responsible of this change or justify myself by saying that I lack the time for my other projects. Still, my goal will not come true and everything would stay the same. One option that we all have is to act out of fear of someone else's opinions or fear of being fired for not doing what we are asked to, but these are reactions and in the long term it will foster fatigue and boredom. Nobody likes to work unwillingly.

As a Huge Company employee, was it my obligation to make these changes? After all, it is their very processes what make things the way they are. It is my duty to follow those processes to the T. On a closer look, Huge Company does not exist on its own, but rather that it is made up of individuals. We are in fact the ones who decide the ways

---

6   https://responsibility.com/responsibility—process/

of Huge Company. Should I do what these individuals ask of me or should I do what I think is best for me and for us? I can also drop this challenge, give up and resign. Ultimately, it is a decision.

But I had learned a lot. I was positive that if I managed to make a change and do things differently, we could see improvements that would translate into personal achievements. I would have tools to meet my expectations, both personal and professional. I did not have all the answers, but I knew we could do better. Surely there would be very good ideas and I wanted to take full responsibility for them. I wanted to be part of that change.

I returned home full of energy. The flight seemed really fast and I was happy that my family and friends received me. And like any good Mexican, we went for tacos for dinner.

We're back. Now what?

*The real voyage of discovery consists not in seeking
new landscapes, but in having new eyes.*
—Marcel Proust

Back at Huge Company on Monday, I met with Jaime
and Daisy at the cafeteria. I told them broadly what I had
learned and how we could use it. It was rewarding to share
these ideas with my team during breakfast, and I think

companies should encourage this: **there should be a space where teams can get together and horizontally discuss a subject.** This would nurture the first value of agility: "Individuals and interactions over processes and tools".

We were finishing breakfast when my phone rang. It was the Chief. He wanted to know if I had a few minutes to talk about the trip.

"Sure" I said. "What would be a good time?"

"I am with Ángel at a meeting room. Can you join us?"

I grabbed my stuff and I ran to the meeting room. The Chief greeted me with a hearty handshake. "It's good to have you back!" That made me feel good, like I was valuable for my team. It is fascinating how powerful communication is, and how recognition or words of encouragement can change your day.

Ángel and I began explaining what we had learned, not just about the tool, but also about the Agile Manifesto, its principles and values. We went into detail about the framework, the ways in which we could apply it, and finally, how this tool could be useful to us. We did a demonstration using the information derived from the training.

The Chief listened attentively, nodding in a way I interpreted as approval. From time to time, he would utter an "I see" or "okay". After 45 minutes, the Chief wanted to know only two things: "Can this tool be used in our distribution departments?" We answered affirmatively in unison. "What do we need for more people to know and use the Agile Manifesto?" Ángel and I looked at each other: we had no idea.

I remembered the task we had been given, and I thought we could use this opportunity. I told the Chief about agile coaches and explained a possible course of action would be talking to them to learn about their own process. The Chief accepted our proposal and we got to work.

We knew we could not do this on our own, so we recruited more people. I was certain we could count on Daysi and Jaime, but we needed others as well. There was someone else who collaborated every time his busy schedule allowed for it; we will call him the Viking. He, too, was a manager and kept contact with the agile coaches, so he introduced us and we proposed a collaboration.

In retrospective, this group of people makes me think that, without intending to, we were following the eight steps of John Kotter's change model:[7]

1. Create a sense of urgency: speak with upper management about the advantages these changes would have in order to get them involved.
2. Build a guiding coalition: create a common front within the organization, that shares the same vision and supports change; it is best if this group belongs to multiple departments or teams.

---

7   https://www.kotterinc.com/

3. Form a strategic vision: elaborate a clear vision that is easy to share in order to avoid any resistance to change.
4. Communicate the vision: this project for change needs to be shared with the entire organization; leaders must be consistent and preach by example.
5. Enable action by removing barriers: it is necessary to empower and support people for them to be able to eliminate obstacles.
6. Generate short—term wins: establish a series of short—term objectives that can lead you to guaranteed success and serve as an example to motivate improvement during this change process.
7. Sustain acceleration: changing things is not enough, it is necessary to have a plan for continuous improvement.
8. Institute change: create a culture of change within the company.

By then we had created a sense of urgency and we were about to build a coalition for change. We had a call with the agile coaches and they agreed to come over. In the meantime, we would get everything ready to greet them, like preparing meeting rooms, organizing a schedule and calendars. The idea was to have brief talks and courses in which they could share what agility meant, its benefits, and a little help building the frameworks. They would also hold meetings with the coalition so we could start implementing the agile work process.

It was an intense week since we had our everyday work, our formative meetings with the agile coaches and the meetings where we would design the strategy to follow.

One of our agile coaches was BeeGee, so I tried to make the most of his visit. I learned a lot of Kanban from him and he showed me different exercises[8] to understand the workflow and encourage collaboration.

Most of our coworkers preferred Scrum and we started to consider whether to pay for certified learning. I was happy about the possibilities. It had been a long time since I had received any training from the company I worked for. This was an exciting moment, and it was only going getting better...

After a few weeks, once the agile coaches had left, every member of the coalition had certain extra activities to promote change in our ways of work. The vision of "becoming agile" was communicated across the company, but we were missing the next steps. We had to empower people to get short–term results and prove this type of work process truly works, so some members of the coalition undertook specific projects in which we would implement what we had learned and assume a leadership role.

I kept my role as a technical leader for my three projects. At times I would provide some input as an agile coach when

---

8 https://fullmetalagilist.wordpress.com/2020/04/08/simulaciones-kanban-a-distancia/

helping the Scrum masters, who were former business ana-
lysts. Together, we were looking for ways to run retrospectives, refinement the backlog and communicate our findings
to the technical team. This helped me understand both perspectives a little better. But since the coalition wanted to
demonstrate the empowerment and results agile practices
could achieve, we had to lead a project or team fully using an
agile framework or process. From the options available, the
lion's share were new projects where we would use Scrum,
but I was looking for something where I would have the freedom to lean on Kanban. I talked it over with the coalition and
the Chief thought it was just what we needed.

Within Huge Company, the Production department
produced an incident report and the related costs. If possible, the support team tried to find root solutions. But
there were usually so many incidents that they never
had time to run an analysis and find root causes, much
less a permanent solution. With this issue in mind, the
Chief suggested forming a team fully dedicated to solving these incidents at their root and, in this way, reduce
our downtime. After discussing the matter, we arrived
at these decisions:

- The systems would be prioritized according to the impact these incidents had. The team should have the
  power to investigate the impact, define the priority
  and find a solution.

- The team members would be fully dedicated to investigate, develop, solve, and rollout these changes.
- The team's progress would be measured by the impact on the systems, not by the changes made.
- The team would decide on the framework they found most convenient.
- Our work cadence would be every two weeks, but progress reports would be produced monthly.

Once we agreed on these points, I accepted the Chief's proposal. As I left the office, I realized something. On paper, everything looked grand, but something was missing. Who would be part of the team, and where would I find its members?

I choose you!

If you want to go fast, go alone; if you
want to go far, go together.
—African proverb

In the following days, I devoted part of my time to finding members for the "Fix it" team. I knew I would need people with different backgrounds, most of them technical, but knowledgeable about the different systems within Huge

Company. So I went around looking for the best candidates. At each department that owned a system I sold the idea of reducing incidents, finding root solutions and providing regular maintenance for their applications. They loved the idea, but were unwilling to commit people unless it were for emergencies.

Only the support team would commit one girl, who we will call Swan. She had been working in the support department for a couple of years now, and was looking for a change. She had technical expertise and knew the rollout and support processes by heart. I soon discovered she was considered "problematic" because she wanted a change, and that was the reason she was allowed to work in the "Fix it" team.

Swan and I went to the Chief's office and asked for his help since the "Fix it" team consisted of only two people. His initial reaction was anger, and a bit of disappointment, which I believe is common to rejection. I thought about why **it is important to have the support of people in decision–making and influential roles for any sort of transformation. It is not enough to share a vision: human, financial and time resources are needed in order to make it happen.** Having the Chief's support was a relief, but we needed greater influence in other departments if we were to count on their cooperation and get the people with the background we needed to achieve our goals. Which weren't *our* goals, but common to the organization.

Working on silos gives the impression that there is competition between departments.

Lacking the human resources, the Chief checked the budget. There was enough for three agents through an external consultant. This was both good and bad. We now had three people fully dedicated to the team, and since they were new, their work process could be more easily molded to our needs. But on the other hand, due to budget limitations they would be fresh out of university; evidently, having no prior work experience, we had a learning curve ahead.

I remembered that phrase from *Ratatouille:* "The world is often unkind to a new talent, new creations... The new needs friends". Within Huge Company, a lot of departments were unkind to this new way of working. We needed friends, and these came as new people, who also needed friends. **We had to create a safe environment and a sense of teamwork between us, as well as making clear how we would work and the benefits that agile values and principles brought along.**

With the arrival of "Ed", "Edd" and "Eddie", Swan and I organized workshops where we explained our work process and which systems needed fixing. While Swan showed them where to find the servers, logins, databases, codes and locations, I explained the Agile Manifesto: its values and principles, as well as Kanban practices. We also developed simulations using our context at Huge Company. One week later, Ed, Edd and Eddie were ready to start.

I asked the Chief for a place where the five of us could work together and sit as close as possible to foster collaboration. I also asked for a board or at least a wall to take notes. The only place the Chief could offer was a common area known as Almoloyita.[9] Everything was ready:

---

9   The Federal Social Readaptation Center No. 1 "Altiplano" is Mexico's most secure federal prison, infamous for the escape of Joaquín "El Chapo" Guzmán in 2015. Prior to taking its current name, the facility was first named after the municipality where it is located, Almoloya de Juárez. —Trans. note.

we had the people, a workspace, and a little training. It was time to get cracking.

And then I started doubting. How do I start working with Kanban?

Systemic think... what was that again?

The definition of insanity is doing the same thing over and over and expecting different results.
—Attributed to Albert Einstein

I asked BeeGee for advice on how to get started with Kanban. He suggested to begin with STATIK (System Thinking Approach To Implement Kanban), a workshop consisting of six basic steps usually applied iteratively to explore the correct design of the system. STATIK is not designed for a single—step sequential process, but instead is built to work like a feedback loop.

These are the six steps:

1. Identify the source of dissatisfaction
2. Analyze the demand
3. Analyze the capabilities
4. Model the workflow
5. Identify the classes of service
6. Design the Kanban system

The "Fix it" team gathered for a small workshop. Two hours later, we had arrived to our Kanban system, which in hindsight was very austere. My core learnings were these:

- Given we lacked a perspective from all the departments with which we collaborated, we did not understand the interactions.
- We only devoted two hours to this process since we had the pressure to get to work.
- Since this was a new team, we did not have a well—established workflow. We thought we could define it, but in reality we would to have to adapt to the rollout flow in place.

The result was something like this:

	To do	Doing	Done
Payments			
Credit			
Income			
Other			
Stoppers			

Our "WIP limit" would be focusing on the top three systems with more incidents. The flow we were interested in was the code we would modify in order to solve incidents, which would be considered complete at release. We would also hold our daily 15—minute sessions at our board in Almoyolita. Every two weeks we would examine each system to check the total number of incidents, prioritize them and focus our efforts on them during the next two weeks. After the release, we would have a small retrospective.

As we used this system, we started seeing issues we had not anticipated. Ed, Edd and Eddie kept competing so they could brag who had more items. At some point they thought that they would be praised for having a lot of work on their hands, while in fact we cared more about finishing those tasks. This has a strong connection with a phrase every Kanbanist worth their salt knows: "stop starting, start finishing".

We had to change the items from "codes being modified" to "incident being solved", so that solving an incident seen in each system consisted of multiple codes.

This also encouraged collaboration, since it was likely that Ed, Edd and Eddie were working on solving a Payments incident which involved two different codes with a common goal.

This is another advantage of Kanban: the system and the process can change along the way. This promotes evolutive change and continuous improvement. As we uncovered our workflow and dissatisfactions, we aimed for improvement and simplifying the process. This reduces the time and cost that can derive from micromanagement or excessive control over a process. One advantage of being a self–managed team is that it can define its processes.

And so went by the first two weeks we had set to reduce the number of incidents in the Payments system of Huge Company. We had agreed that we would complete it in this period, so we made changes to the code, run tests, asked for authorizations, transferred the code to the release department and then went into production.

Every Monday we would receive a report with the Huge Company's systems incidents. We were excited to see the impact of our changes. It was indeed a nice surprise to see the incidents had diminished in comparison with an average weekend. We were proud of what we had accomplished.

When I showed it to the Chief, he told me it was a sign we were working. "But what's the end goal? Just diminishing...? Any team can do that. Set an goal, a percentage, and see what you can do to achieve it. Do you think you can lower the number of incidents by 80%?"

That hit me like a ton of bricks. I went back to the "Fix it" team and told them what the Chief had said. Some of them disliked it, but I think he was right. We needed a goal, we couldn't just work for the sake of it. So, we met to plan the next two weeks. This time, the team decided to not just take in Payments activities, but also consider the Credit and Income systems. We wanted to prove we could reduce that percentage. Our ambition was so great that we lowered the numbered of released codes.

The question was why. How come the more we decided to do, the less results we were turning in? I talked it over with BeeGee, and he explained the concept of "limiting the work in progress". I told him we were trying by choosing only a few systems, but he kept stressing that was just one way of doing things: the problem was we did not know how many codes the team was modifying in parallel. When we checked the amount of work under the "Doing" column, we realized that the five people on the team were modifying 18 codes, roughly four codes each. This felt normal, but BeeGee explained that in fact it meant that each of us had three times as many chances of multitasking.

Humans are capable of properly working on a single task at a time. As more tasks are parallelized, the quality of the work will suffer and the time these tasks take to complete will increase. In software development, ours is known as "knowledge work". It is similar to being a craftsman, since no two codes are alike. A programmer's creativity, knowledge and ability to address complexity play an important role. This makes it necessary to focus on a single activity or foster collaboration, as two heads are always better than one. However, this is usually perceived as "wasteful" because if I have five people at my disposal, they should be working on five different things. But since software is knowledge work, collaboration increases creativity and reduces multitasking.

This is one reason why Kanban limits the amount of work in progress to strengthen collaboration. We decided to limit the amount of work like this: every two weeks we would review only the two most important systems; out of those, we would review the incidents and choose only 14 codes. That way, each one would have three items on their list, and whoever had two could help someone else.

The result was satisfactory for the Payments system, but in Credit we only reduced 20% of the incidents. We had a meeting with the Support team and asked for a weekly report with the number of incidents that the systems generated in order to understand how the reports of these developed and prioritize accordingly. Instead of working based on what someone else's requests, we used data for better decision—making and focusing on our goal of reducing 80% of the incidents in such a way that we would work less whilst obtaining better results. Once we applied these changes, the Payments system began stabilizing, which allowed us to shift our priorities. We started working on the Income system and lowered the priority on Payments.

It was a good month, and we were seeing the results. In our retrospective meetings, the team showed commitment and interest. One of our agreements was to share knowledge on certain systems, so the proposal was as follows: by limiting the amount of work in process to someone available, that person would have the chance to work with somebody engaged with a system they might be interested in learning about. We know that this causes a learning curve generates and a slight gap in productivity, but after a while this stabilizes and productivity even increases. We knew we would have to commit and, on occasions, work a few extra hours to try and make up for that curve.

What mattered about our retrospective meetings was that any action taken was not imposed, but an initiative that came from the team. This drives commitment and a culture of constant improvement. We also had breakfast as a team, although this usually happened on weekends, in order to relax for at least an hour. Ed, Edd and Eddie were new, and I did not know Swan that well. **Teambuilding demands some time to establish trust within the group.** Knowing who to trust, who to rely on, and having the openness to say "I don't know" and ask for help is very important for a team. It is unusual for a work relationship to grow into considering your coworkers as friends, but we can influence to make it happen. It is not essential, but it helps collaboration and creativity happen naturally, without feeling forcing the thing.

In a nutshell, from our perspective the "Fix it" team was doing great, but we were about to face the greatest challenge yet. We had been summoned by the executive committee to show our progress...

The fear of being graded

Not everyone's so bad, not everything is wrong
Not everyone is a villain who wants you hung
—Fobia, "Hoy tengo miedo"

The Chief told us that he wanted to show our progress with using Kanban in a meeting with the executive board of Huge Company. The team was excited. I was terrified. I tend to worry too much and be overly apprehensive about my day to day, whether it is work—related or personal. My first and only meeting with the board had not been the best. A few years ago, I was called for a quality evaluation. At that time, I was very "critical", almost negative I'd say. Not everyone likes to be told what they are doing wrong, and my biggest mistake was phrasing things very harshly. Worst of all, I would point out the problems, but fail to give solutions.

Giving feedback requires not just a critical personality, but also an environment to speak honestly. Both the feedback giver and receiver need empathy as much as openness. When I vented about bad planning or a senseless request, it was not taken kindly. That is why I was asked to change my ways. I complied, but there was never a follow—up. As a result, I had to switch to a different department. I did not trust the executive board.

From this experience, I learned that my feedback needed a certain structure and a goal: it must provide mutual support and change in time, it must be close to the event discussed, specific, concise, not forced and close by asking the opinion of the person receiving the feedback.

Nowadays, I express what I see. Based on those observations, I detail my thoughts or ideas and share my feelings around the fact. Lastly, I state what I am looking for, what can change or the ways in which I can help.

For example, when preparing the presentation for the executive board, I gave this feedback to the "Fix it" team:

- I have noticed we have discussed a lot about what we will present (what I see).
- If we don't make a decision, we won't finish on time (my ideas and thoughts).
- I think that if we delay this any longer, we'll rush this through and the presentation will be lacking in quality (my emotions and feelings).
- I would like to focus on two slides as a viable minimum, and then build on top; I can work on one of these slides (what I am looking for and how can I help).

To begin work on the presentation for the meeting, we had a brainstorming session: it is best to start with multiple perspectives, always keeping an eye on a common goal. Our challenge was what information we could include in only two slides. We knew that in order to make an effective presentation there should be as little text as possible in a slide. The person giving the presentation must guide the conversation and rely on images only if there are numbers involved. Jeff Bezos, the founder of Amazon, forbids the use of PowerPoint [10] since it lacks context. Still, we had to present something.

I asked BeeGee for help, and he in turn asked me this: "What do you want the board to see, and what do you want

---

10 https://forbes.co/dos0dos0/08/dos1/actualidad/jeff-bezos-prohibe-usar-powerpoint-en-reuniones-de-amazon/

from it?" I wanted them to see the work we had done, our results and how much better we could be if we had the support of the Production department, for both rollouts and incidents.

BeeGee suggested creating metrics based on our outcomes (the percentage of incident reduction). We could use a cumulative flow diagram to show our work rhythm and visualize the bottlenecks derived from the dependency from Production. That way, we could close the presentation by stating that in order to get better results, we needed support from other departments.

The outcomes report was fairly simple to create, all we did was a weekly comparison of the incidents report we were sent, showing how a decreased with every release. A simple bar graph was enough. The actual challenge was the cumulative flow diagram. I had heard of it, but never done one. BeeGee helped me by explaining and sharing examples, but it all depended on us since he was not readily available.

To make the flow diagram, we used our board. Thanks to our daily sessions, we had a spreadsheet where we counted the number of items we had worked on for each system, all timestamped and with their corresponding status. Building this table is useful to show our workflow, what we have yet to do, where are the bottlenecks and how long it takes us to finish each item.

In one simple graph, we can learn three important metrics:

- The lead time is how long it takes for a work item to pass through the system from beginning to end.
- The delivery rate is how many work items were finished within a certain amount of time, for example, the number of codes we delivered every two weeks.
- The work in progress (WIP) is the total amount of items in a system (or a part of it) at a given time.

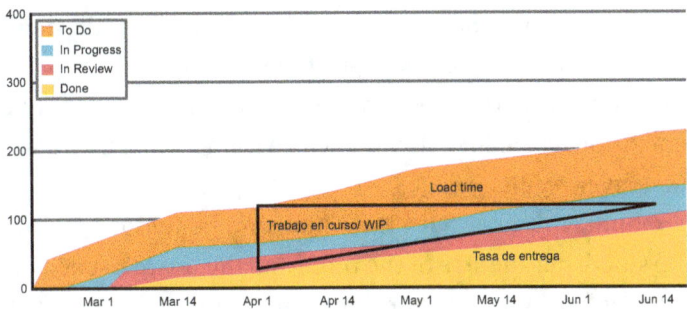

Thanks to the diagram, we already had two metrics regarding our progress. As for the results, they could be found in the incidents reports. We only needed to clarify what kind of support we needed for the next steps.

Through our metrics we noticed it took us two weeks on average to deliver the 14 codes we modified to reduce incidents. However, upon closer look, we also noticed they waited for approval at least one day because we depended on the Release department to rollout into production. We stated this finding on the third slide: being dependent on the Rollout team created a waiting time of at least one day. Our proposal was to onboard a coworker from the Release department into team, so we could rollout once the code was ready.

We now had a simple way to show our work. Everybody worked on the presentation, and by the end we were happy with the results.

But faced our first major issue. Only one of us would be allowed into the meeting, which seemed unfair since we all had pitched in. I was pretty upset. The person going in that meeting room would be perceived as the face of the operation, when in reality the whole team had worked hard to deliver results.

I talked it over with the Chief, and he told me he understood, but the size of the room and the board's schedule made it hard for five people to stand there. "Imagine what would happen if every team asked for the same thing. The meetings would be packed." I understood that a team needs a proper space to showcase their work to stakeholders, rather than being held accountable and asking for feedback and help. The whole team should be present since this is a joint effort, more so if it would be praised. The Chief told me he would try to hold monthly sessions where all teams could show their achievements, but it would be their responsibility to make the most of the sessions so they would not become monotonous.

Back with the "Fix it" team, I delivered the news. Only one of us would go to the meeting. I did not want to be that person, and thought Swan was better suited for it since she had more expertise. Being new and lacking the confidence, Ed, Edd and Eddie were the first to take a step back. That was the reason I wanted them to go in with someone else, so they could learn. Swan said I was the best fit since I had the Chief's support and understood the metrics better than anybody. I tried to change her mind by pointing out she was more knowledgeable about the processes and that she would be able to answer the more technical questions. In the end, we decided to take a vote and the result was unanimous. Everyone wanted me to go.

I had a bittersweet feeling. I was happy that the team trusted me, but I also thought I was the one who least deserved it. I was probably experiencing imposter syndrome. After deciding, I let the Chief know we were ready, and he told me to email the assistant director telling him I'd be going to the meeting and attach the presentation.

The ritual you have to follow in order to schedule a meeting with a director is fascinating. This should be simpler to encourage straightforward communication. While it does not always flow properly, these gatekeepers slow things down and hinders conversations simply because it is a pain to have to look for people and schedule a meeting.

After sending the meeting request and the presentation, it was just a matter of waiting. By the time the day arrived, I had not worn a suit and a tie in years at Huge Company. I have always thought you should not judge a book by its cover, more so if we all work in an organization under the same values, culture and purpose. Sure, I had no intention of showing up in my underwear, but I was thinking of dressing more casually, so as to show my reluctance to wearing a tie and a shirt just because somebody up in the hierarchy would be there.

Daysi, on the other hand, had a different opinion. She said I had every right to dress however I wanted, but I had to keep in mind the end goal of this meeting. If my purpose was to gain allies, I had to build empathy not just in the results and the content of the presentation, but also towards my own personality. If a first impression lasts forever, then it should better be as relatable as possible. The board would likely see me under a different light if I stepped off their customs, and more often than not, being different has a negative impact in perception. If I showed up as they expected me to, they would be more relaxed, and it would be easier to build rapport by being a part of their group. Maybe later on I would be able to have a more relaxed attitude.

While we all have principles and values we are not willing to give up, at times they are nothing but whims, in my opinion. In this case, I could change my attire in order to get a better impression.

It was my first time at the corporate offices of Huge Company. It was a whole other world and not just because it was brand new, or because the cafeteria offered sushi, but because the work spaces were open and collaborative. Where I worked, the departments was separated from each other by room dividers, and it was not really allowed to hang anything on the walls; if we did, the janitors would take it down. When we began the "Fix it" team, we used Almoloyita because it had the space, open areas where we could be together and a wall in which to hang our board.

At the board's building there were many areas that followed this layout, round or movable tables for whole teams and boards to draw on. Instead of cubicles, there were collaborative spaces with sofas and network nodes. Spaces like this encourage collaboration and communication, and I thought that teams need places where they can talk without having to book a meeting room. **If we are trying to boost collaboration, creativity and participation, we should ask ourselves how much our environment encourages that.**

I went to the cafeteria, bought a coffee and walked towards the meeting room, where I found five people. It was a big room that could host fifteen people. One by one, the members of the executive board walked in. The Chief arrived and I noticed his "you can do this" look.

The meeting began. The first manager discussed his project: the progress achieved and how everything was in due course. After fifteen minutes, I noticed there were twenty slides in his presentation. It seemed odd to me, but I lacked the context to judge the thing. Being the first speaker, I thought it must have been an important project; on the other hand, he had taken 30 minutes out of the hour we had scheduled. He finished by requesting an adjustment in the plan's scope, which meant a bigger budget and more time.

The board asked questions like who designed the plan, why it hadn't been checked, and who was in charge of performance improvements. They agreed to have a follow-up meeting to answer these questions and present an action plan. Oh, sweet, sweet irony! A meeting to plan a meeting! Forty minutes had gone by and four more people were in line.

The next manager had 15 slides in his presentation; after 15 minutes, he had shown five. The meeting had to be extended. Obviously, nobody would admit to more important things to do than sitting before the board. Somebody picked up a phone and asked an assistant to add an extra hour, and that was that.

I started to panic when I saw the third manager had eleven slides. I only had three, and was sure I would be the laughingstock. Maybe it was a common thing to have a lot to say to the board. I opened my laptop and tried to find ways to add some slides, but at the same time I felt ashamed for not paying attention. The fourth manager had thirteen slides. At this point, I felt like I was in Shark Tank and my pitch was way too short. I tried to get the Chief's attention: I wanted him to see my panicked expression and do something, but he was either focused on the presentations or on his phone.

Finally, it was my turn. I took a deep breath, got up and plugged my laptop to the projector. Remote control in hand, I began. "I will be brief" were my first words, and they surely were true. I explained the benefits that the "Fix it" team had over the past month. I showed the graph and discussed the decrease in incidents. Then I showed the cumulative flow diagram and underlined our timeline and the bottlenecks we faced. To wrap up, I presented our needs and our proposal to onboard someone from the Rollout team in order to reduce the dependency on them, a step which would increase our collaboration.

The whole presentation took me five minutes or less. The room was silent. I felt like the biggest fraud ever. While everyone else took at least 25 minutes, I made them waste their time. I couldn't even look at the Chief straight in the face. The head of the Rollout department broke the silence. "Please send me the presentation, so I can check the figures and define the headcount you need."

He asked the Chief if he had a candidate. He said he didn't because this was the first time we discussed this. He then looked at me and asked if we needed anything else. "Not at the moment. Thank you for your attention."

The meeting finished one hour later than planned. I approached the Chief and apologized, telling him there was not enough material for the meeting and that it had been too short. He smirked at me and said this situation could have been resolved with an email; however, they tend to dismiss requests like ours unless you pitch it to the board. "You did great. You were brief and to the point. In fact, you caught their eye and made something happen. Now comes the hard part: sending the presentation, answering their questions and reaching your goals. This was only a first step, but it was a good first step."

I have noticed a tendency to be overly pessimistic, or at least I feel like that a lot. We have yet to do the things we set out to do and we already feel defeated. That is why we tend to avoid doing them. After this experience, I began trusting myself a little more. Whenever things seem too complicated, I try to see which allies I could count on. In this particular meeting, I forgot about the Chief and that he would have my back in case something went wrong. Also, he would not have taken me to the meeting if he did not trust me. It is very important to have people we can rely on. **The companies where we work depend on interpersonal and even political relations. At the end of the day, they are made up of people who can help us reach our goals.**

You don't have to be best friends with the person whose help you need, but they should be someone with whom you can talk more candidly at work. That way, you will be able to understand their needs and align them with your own. Before I understood how these relations worked, I never attended the end–of–year parties at Huge Company, much less the smaller department get—togethers. At best I would go out on weekends with Daysi and Jaime, whom I consider my friends, or had breakfast with the "Fix it" team. Ever since this experience, I started showing up to more work–related events.

Back in Almoloyita, I told the team how had things turned out. They were very excited, and made fun of me for our three slides in comparison with the other managers' 20.

I would have loved for the entire team to be there: I would have felt more at ease. Although the Chief's support was good enough, I realized that when you have a good team, you try to share those times with them. After some more talking and joking, Swan suggested we should go out. We agreed unison, checked what we still had to do and took 30 minutes to finish off any urgent tasks. I ran back to my place to send the presentation to the head of the Rollout department, whom we will now call "Mr. Ride or Die".

The team met at the parking lot and headed towards the nearest bar. We spent the rest of the evening telling stories, making fun of each other and dreaming about the future. That day, we felt like champions. We had passed the first test. It was time to celebrate and enjoy this small triumph.

The sun always shines after the storm

I firmly believe that any man's finest hour, the greatest fulfillment of all he holds dear, is that moment when he has worked his heart out in a good cause and lies exhausted on the field of battle, victorious.
 —Vince Lombardi

A week had gone by after the meeting with the board. We had not heard from Mr. Ride or Die, but we kept on working. I was focused on my other projects, which, to be honest, I had left to the side since they showed little progress, unlike my situation with the "Fix it" team. Luckily there were more people working on them.

Around that time, I got an email with a notice about my accumulated vacation days. In Mexico, workers get six days of paid vacation after the first year, adding one extra day per year worked. I had been part of Huge Company for almost five years and I had not used all the vacation days I had earned. It is the company's policy that, after a given time, unused vacation days were lost. The email indeed reminded me of the policy. I got worried because I had to take those days off, right now that the team was progressing and I still had to work on my other projects.

I asked Jaime how to handle this, and he simply said: "You should always give yourself time to rest." It was an easy thing for him to say, but I felt it would be irresponsible to take time off at that moment. Daysi chipped in and asked when was the last time I had taken five days for myself.

"If we consider the times I'd ask for three days before or after long weekends, I actually did it only a few months ago."

Daysi was not impressed. She meant five days straight apart from weekends.

"You need a long rest, you deserve it".

Jaime added that it was critical for my mind and body to rest, since my performance was dropping. It is always important to give your brain a break: **like any other machine, if it works at a 100% of its capacity it will burn out, and then the body gets sick, you suffer muscle pain or simply stress.** I understood all of these, and obviously thought they were important, but I did not feel like this was a good time to go. As I said, I felt it would have been irresponsible to leave everything. On the other hand, I was scared that me taking time off would be considered unethical; and while by law they could not deny the request, I might have to face the consequences once I came back.

This was a trust issue that the environment in Huge Company created for me. Daysi and Jaime stopped me and asked me why I thought that. I had never actually gone through something like that: these were merely beliefs of mine. My own fears, prejudice and imaginary scenarios built a fictitious reality. However, I also think it is important for Huge Company to create a safe environment where one can ask such things.

On that regard, psychological safety at work means having an environment where people can safely express their ideas or concerns, ask questions, and share their mistakes without fearing retaliation or being humiliated or judged. The fact I could talk to Daysi and Jaime was because I trusted them and I knew there would be no consequences, but I was still scared of discussing it with anybody else, to the extremes of not taking time off.

Daysi suggested having a conversation with the Chief, now that he had seen my good work and communication was better. I would obviously have to lay the facts so he knew my absence would not be an issue. She also suggested I find a backup that could look after my activities in the meantime, and write an out–of–office message letting senders know my responses would be slower, but could contact someone else in my absence. Finally, I should block my calendar and mark it accordingly so I couldn't be scheduled into a meeting. This way, I would be able to relax.

A safety environment, on the other hand, must also consider that if a person takes time off, there will be no great changes, and that the only way of achieving this is sharing and collaborating. That said, I asked Swan if she could be my backup while I was gone, and she agreed. All I had to do was explain how to access the incidents reports, which was pretty straightforward.

I met Seb to ask for his approval. First, I updated him about the projects, and explained there were a lot of things that needed information. The technical part, specifically the databases that were my responsibility, would be overseen by other people in the team, whom I had already asked for help. His answer sounded like something my father would have said: "I do not know, it depends on the Chief".

This seemed like a subtle way of denying any responsibility, but I think it was part of that fear atmosphere at Huge Company around being accountable for certain decisions.

It is possible Seb did not want to approve anything without the Chief's consent out of fear that something might go wrong in my absence. If he said the Chief had agreed on this, he would be covered.

To avoid having an unnecessary argument, I went to see the Chief right away. When I told him I wanted to take some time off, he said: "Why are you asking me? Isn't this something Seb should approve?" I told him he had directed me to ask for his authorization as well. The Chief nodded lightly and chuckled sarcastically. Rather than disapproval, it was more like he was saying: "Now I have to cover for him again", but that might just be me, so I will never know for sure.

The Chief asked me about my workload, if someone would be my backup and if there was anything urgent or that needed special attention while I was gone. I told him we were expecting a response from Mr. Ride or Die, and he told me not to worry. He then sent an email to Seb letting him know he approved eight days of vacation for me. I thanked him for his trust and support. Before I could leave, he told me that it was good to take the eight days and come back midweek. I asked him why, since I would rather be back on a Monday in order to work the full week.

"When you come back on Monday, your mind and body think: 'After some rest, I'll have to wait another week to rest again'. And so you get to the office anxious. Instead, if you come back on Wednesday or Thursday, it is just one or two days till you can rest again and this relaxes you."

As I said, experience and knowledge are only useful if they are shared. I went back to my station, told Swan my vacation had been authorized starting next week. I had three days to prepare everything. I called my girlfriend to decide on a destination. I have always enjoyed the process of planning holidays, and these were the very first that would be that long. I thought it would be complicated, but it turns out when you do something with hopeful anticipation, it is actually simple, and you invest all of your time and energy on it. We decided to go to Huatulco, and since I wanted complete relaxation, we decided to fly to avoid driving on the highway. The flight lasted an hour and a half, which was perfect for us.

While packing my bags, I was to take the company's laptop when my girlfriend pointed out I did not need it if I had left everything ready. I told her it was just in case something urgent came up, or if I needed to check something. The expression on her face told me she disagreed: "I do not think that would be real rest, since you are still engaged with work".

Nowadays, it is actually more difficult than ever to disconnect from work, and this means it is all the more necessary to do it. The pandemic brought us home office, but we also need to learn to take our focus away from work and enjoy a good rest at the end of the day, not to mention if we are going on holidays.

Her remark made me think if I really needed to bring my laptop with me. Was I doing this because I did not trust my team? Or because I was scared that I would not be available if they needed me? As I pondered these questions, I realized I was indeed afraid of not being available, but my team, whom I trusted, would be. I was thinking about this when my girlfriend said: "I do not want to minimize your work, but you seriously cannot disconnect just eight days? What's going to happen if you do? Is Huge Company going to explode?"

She was right. I was part of Huge Company, but nothing would happen if I took time off to rest, to recover, to take care of myself. We worry a lot about our professional development, but personal development should include caring for ourselves. I took the laptop out of the bag, and although I was a little nervous about it at first, I felt better with time.

During the trip, I thought that vacations are very important for everyone, especially high–performance teams. One of the principles of the Agile Manifesto is that: "Agile processes promote sustainable development. The sponsors, developers, and users should be able to maintain a constant pace indefinitely." I then understood that in order to maintain a constant pace indefinitely, it must be sustained, and for that, it is important to note that capacity is finite, especially the human capacity to respond to a certain workload.

In order for pace to be constant and keep development sustainable, it is necessary to rest from time to time. Otherwise the team and its members will suffer from stress. A high—performance team does not take less time off and work longer hours: they are efficient without burdening themselves. To this end, it is important to work smart.

This reminds me of another principle: "Simplicity is the art of maximizing the amount of work not done". We usually think that we need to be busy or work a lot just for the sake of it. We feel like we will earn a prize or an accolade because of our effort. At Huge Company, whenever I left at the end of my workday, some people told me: "Only half a day today?" Or when I stayed longer they said: "Leaving already? If they do not see you giving 100%, you won't get a promotion". This needs to change. We need to start encouraging teams to complete their work without the need of extra time.

For me, being able to go on holidays without having to worry was an achievement, and I felt very excited about whatever came next. It was a well—deserved reward, and I was fully committed to share it with the team. As soon as I came back, I made sure they took some time off.

Back and trying my best

We might not be perfect, but we can always be better.
—Anonymous

Back from my holidays, Swan updated me on the news. Mr. Ride or Die had finally answered. In his email he asked about our delivery times, capacity and metrics. We knew we needed to collaborate with the Rollout department, but we did not know exactly the steps or processes our deliverables followed. We had to act fast, or else lose momentum, so we held another STATIK meeting to reassess what we had learned. We invited people from the Rollout department to explain the process they followed.

In the "Model the workflow" phase, we asked what they did once we delivered the codes. This is important because even if it seems like we do different things because we belong to different areas, these relations must be considered as a joint service. The "Fix it" team solved incidents, but it depended on other areas to deliver the service. The Rollout team focused on other teams' releases, but it needed their input. Looking at the different teams as a network of interconnected services provides a clearer image. So this STATIK session provided us with more information. We then learned that they took the programs for rollout at most one day before their due date. They made backups, delete everything and move the programs to their destination. This told us their job took them at least a day of the fifteen days we had planned in our workflow.

At the beginning, we were trying to figure out how to make this process transparent and visible to everyone. One suggestion was to make a board for the Rollout department where they could use Kanban for their services and pending tasks. This seemed like the smarter choice, since we would work in a similar way.

I talked it over with the Chief, and he said expanding the agile method to other areas sounded interesting, but I had to see if it was sustainable since we had to offer training, tracking and support. It was not merely a matter of explaining how things worked and then leaving them to fend for themselves. The Chief asked me to develop an action plan to make this transition.

I talked to BeeGee and asked him for advice. Together we made the plan and looked at dates to have a similar training to the one we had abroad, only this time we would be facilitating. I talked this over with Daysi, Jaime and the Viking, who were more than excited to be a part of it. It seemed like all our side work was beginning to come along. We were sharing knowledge and experiences.

For greater drive, I asked everyone to tag along at the meeting with the Chief in order to present the plan. We even asked BeeGee to attend. It was a one–hour meeting; it took us 30 minutes to explain the plan, the other 30 minutes we answered the Chief's questions about schedule, materials and the location for the sessions. The Chief accepted the plan and greenlighted a presentation to the Rollout department. We set up a meeting with them and invited Mr. Ride or Die, but he declined; however, he forwarded it to someone we'll call Iveme.

During the meeting, we discussed the possibility of having the Rollout department work with the agile principles and values whilst relying on the Kanban method. We would provide training, assist them with building the board, hold sessions to encourage collaboration with the "Fix it" team, and give them the agile values and principles.

After the meeting, there was a brief silence. Then Iveme said: "Please send me the presentation, and I'll look it over with Mr. Ride or Die before I give you an answer". I thought about that meme that says "this meeting could have been an email". We just had to send the presentation, without getting an answer or a reaction of any sort. I ignore why most meetings are open to people who lack the knowledge or power to make a decision. This only means the answer will be delayed or the session will have to be repeated. While in every organization there are people in important positions that are unable to attend every meeting (and therefore must prioritize which ones to attend in order to make a decision), meetings that cannot be attended are still important. In such cases, we should rely on our team and delegate these meetings, while granting the team members with decision—making powers. When scheduling meetings, it is important to consider not just the attendees' calendars, but also how much it matters that everyone is present. If this is just an informative meeting, it can be optional, but if decisions are to be made, then attendance should be mandatory.

I went to the Chief and told him what happened. We thought that maybe there would be no changes, or that we had been too drastic with our proposal. Walking in Mr. Ride or Die's shoes, it almost seemed like an invasion.

Without him asking, someone from a different area was telling his team how to do their job better than them. All he asked from us was a little information, nothing more. I think most of us feel this way when someone offers their help without being asked.

When we considered this, we had to change our perspective. I met again with the "Fix it" team to see how we could move on without fully relying on the Rollout department. Our aim was to find a way to show the time it took them to make a release, how many of our codes were waiting for their approval and calculate their capacity. But in order to bring this to light and measure the time, we had to make changes to our board. We added a final column to separate our tasks from pending work from other departments; in this case, that was Rollout.

	To do	Doing	Done	Release
Payments				
Credit				
Income				
Other				
Stoppers				

This way, we could better quantify the work pending release, look at waiting times and ask for help from the Rollout department. This helped me understand a little better the concept of evolutionary change. Unlike a drastic change, evolutionary change is simpler and based on personal needs. This makes it easier to act and sustain. As its name implies, human evolution has taken thousands of years, and while these changes are difficult to perceive, they are necessary for the survival of the species. The same thing goes for **evolution within a company, which entails small sustainable changes that are useful for incremental improvement.**

To begin working on these changes, we developed our own metrics using the cumulative flow diagram. We had meetings with the Rollout department to agree on the programs we would release, align priorities and update our schedules. This provided us with more detailed information we could share with Mr. Ride or Die. After several months, our relation with the Rollout department improved, but our due dates were far from better.

In a retrospective meeting, we discussed the stages of the process that did not show in our board or in the cumulative flow diagram. The Rollout department was not the only area we depended on, and this made us ask wonder how much of our time was our responsibility to manage, and how much of it depended on someone else. And of those dependencies to other areas, how many of them meant a delay?

If we get organized, we'll all win

*Cooperation is the thorough
conviction that nobody can get there
unless everybody gets there.*
—Virginia Burden

We made another STATIK session, this time taking into account the dependencies we had identified in our collaboration with Rollouts. The big difference was that we added specific questions to uncover more about these dependencies and relations with other areas.

- What needs to happen to start this stage?
- What steps do we need to follow to close this stage?
- Are there any other actions after this stage?
- Does this stage depends on our team?
- If this stage does not depend on the team, who is responsible?

We found out we not only depended on the Rollout department. While our job consisted in prioritizing the incidents and sending the codes to production, it was clear there were parts of the process in which we did not participate directly. Thus, we mapped our process under this premise: "All the stages where we can increase capacity and improve delivery time". Having considered that, our job was as follows:

- Prioritize the system we would review
- Select the codes
- Modify the codes
- Test the codes
- Prepare the codes for production testing
- Request authorization regarding change tickets
- Validate changes and follow–up

We knew production testing, authorizing change tickets, code freezing and versioning, and sending to production were part of the process, but we had no influence in them moving faster or with more capacity. All we could do was wait for a response. With this information in mind, we modified our board once more to clarify the process and separate the active work we did from the stages where we waited a response from other areas. This is another example of the evolutionary change that Kanban promotes and why it is better not to get too comfortable with a board, as it will change in and new needs surface.

The end result was this:

	To do	Doing	Done		Release
			Testing	Ticket Release	
Payments					
Credit					
Income					
Other					
Stoppers					

The "Done" column was intended to show where our work was finished; however, it split in the stages that followed: testing, tickets, versioning and rollout.

Our new board was very useful, but still needed a metric for waiting time. After researching the issue, BeeGee suggested exploring the Aging Time metric. This refers to the time elapsed since an item was created. While we had the lead time for each item (which we measured from prioritization to release), there was no distinction between stages or the time we invested on it versus the time that depended on other areas.

At the beginning, the "Fix it" team had numerous complaints. They were afraid that if the metric could be used to quantify the team's or their individual performance, it could be used against them. Swan and I explained that we wanted to know the root cause of our times, and why was it so difficult to speed up the process. We promised them we would not use this tool to compare performance.

I realized **it was crucial to explain why we measure something, what is its importance and the expected benefit.** This is also part of the psychological safety concept. It was necessary for the "Fix it" team to feel safe enough to share what actually happened without having to force anyone to do so. It is vital to have a clear goal that the whole team can understand. In our case, we took the time to make sure everyone felt safe enough to ask as many questions as they needed.

This, in my opinion, is the hardest part of adopting an agile mindset. Critical thinking is crucial, but not for the purpose of finding scapegoats. Instead, the idea is to use collective experience and knowledge, so team members have the freedom to express themselves and improve along with everyone else.

In past experiences it was frowned upon to say that something was not getting done or that it was on hold since it was seen as non–productive time and if that was the case, you were to blame. That's why a lot of people prefer to hide that downtime, and as a result, nothing improves.

If the members of a team do not discuss what is getting worked on in order to improve, they are prone to think "we were better before" with the way they used to work. To encourage conversations about improvement areas, we leaned on the Prime Directive of retrospectives proposed by Norman L. Kerth: "Regardless of what we discover, we must understand and truly believe that everyone did the best job he or she could, given what was known at the time, his or her skills and abilities, the resources available, and the situation at hand."

In this way, we measured the time that our deliverables spent in each stage, and we were able to identify the waiting time that did not depend on us. With this metric, we could determine that our work took five days on average. After that period, it went to the Production and Rollout departments for testing, code freezing, authorizing the change tickets and waiting for the release window. On average, this part took nine days, in which we were unable to help in any way.

We also noticed that this was the waiting time for each code we wanted to release. That meant those nine days were multiplied by each code we modified. For example, if we wanted to reduce the incidents in the Payments system and had to modify one module, we had to check the different codes behind it. It was unlikely we had to work on just one code, and were usually more than two. Therefore, we had to ask the Rollout department to run production tests to measure the impact, and at the same time ask Production for authorization to release these codes once they passed the tests. That required the authorization of the directors of different areas, especially from Support. Thus, for each code we worked on, we had to request testing, raise a change ticket and ask for authorizations. If we finished working on those codes at different moments, the waiting time doubled.

We had considered fifteen days from prioritizing an incident to its release, including the nine days of waiting time. We had to do something to change this if we wanted to reduce our delivery time and become more efficient. We learned this premise from Little's Law, which states that:

Cycle time = Amount of WIP/ Average time to finish

The only way we could be more efficient was reducing the waiting time or prioritizing less tickets to spend more time on less tasks. However, our limitations derived from our dependency on other areas was obvious.

We took this data to the Chief (including our metrics and conclusions) in order to make a plan with his support. Our proposal was to allocate releases every two weeks, as if it was an automatic process. We needed the Production and Rollout teams to get involved, every two weeks, with our releases. This would help cut the waiting time by almost 50%, since instead of raising tickets or waiting for authorizations and testing to be done, we could continue changing the next codes.

We thought we were not asking for much: to have one person from Rollout and one from Production exclusively dedicated to testing our codes, freezing versions and releasing them, every two weeks. Authorizations would already be pre—approved, since all areas would know that every two weeks there would be a window to send those codes to production. It would be like pressing a button every two weeks to release everything without the need of sign—offs or authorizing anything. This was based on the DevOps concept, where the goal is to increase the integration between the development and operations areas, which we were trying to do. However, first we needed to develop this mindset before we could use those tools.

I knew this would mean more responsibility for us, but it was part of the changes we were trying to implement, which would reduce the bureaucracy that slowed us down. The Chief agreed and helped us set a meeting with Mr. Ride or Die, although it would take a month's time due to their busy schedules.

In the meantime I was anxious because it seemed like making improvements was not important, and in consequence the "Fix it" team would not be more efficient, or achieving it would be so difficult that we would need a bigger budget and more people. Hiring more people, on the other hand, did not guarantee an increased productivity since we had to consider the learning curves of new resources and also that communication would become more complex. The Chief's answer was concise: what was important to us might not be to them, or even be troubling for them. We needed to wait before drawing conclusions or pointing the finger.

We waited for a month to talk to Mr. Ride or Die. I discussed this with Daysi, Jaime and the Viking. They had their own problems, and at times we felt overwhelmed, but sharing these experiences helped us think outside the box. Still, we had shared our experiences for so long that they were more cathartic than not, since they did not help us solve our problems. One day, Daysi told us she had been searching for information on agility, and she discovered a community where people gathered to share their experiences with agility in their companies.

Upon further research, we learned the community met the last Thursday of every month. Since it was a free event, the location and the agenda changed from month to month, depending on the availability of speakers or if people were to share their experience using the Lean Coffee technique, which is a structured, but agenda–less meeting. Instead, participants decide the topics through a list of priorities that represents a backlog of subjects. Thus, at the time of the invitation, only the location, time and length are known. This is an easy way of encouraging the exchange of knowledge between the attendees and foster participation in a more active way.

We decided to go, and the experience was very pleasant. We discovered we were not the only ones facing certain problems, and we could give and receive advice to overcome our issues. The conversation topics were diverse, ranging from software development, user experience, design thinking to psychology. The environment was very relaxed, are they always had pizza, beer and people who wanted to talk.

On the other hand, there was always a chance for networking. Imagine having a conversation with the person who designed one of the most famous apps or the tester of a company you follow on social media. This to me became a support group. **It was thinking outside the box, stepping out of your daily work and seeing the situation with new eyes. It was rewarding to get advice from people who did not have our biases, or listening to the experience of someone who had gone through something similar to what we were going through.**

These conversations helped me to prepare for the meeting with Mr. Ride or Die. We found the arguments that would make the proposal more convincing. We felt ready for anything. The meeting was drawing closer, and we would not take a no for an answer.

What? Is this it?

Everything that has a beginning has an ending.
—Anonymous

The meeting with Mr. Ride or Die finally came. It would be simple. One hour, five people. I opened with an explanation as to why we had called for this meeting. I could tell Mr. Ride or Die was interested as I discussed our metrics, waiting time and the dependence with the Production and Rollout departments. As the conversation moved forward, Iveme and Mr. Ride or Die asked questions which I answered with Swan's or the Chief's help.

The issue had been explained, it was time to put forward the solution: "We want to raise a ticket every two weeks in order to make a semiautomatic release of all the codes that are ready." Mr. Ride or Die's face went from interested to angry. He cut me off: "Why do you want to change the ticketing process if it lets us track releases into production?" I explained once again that raising a ticket, asking for authorization, versioning the codes and releasing them took nine days and we wanted to minimize this time to be more efficient.

"But we follow ITIL processes, and they have minimized impacts at release while we can track issues. It helps us be aware of errors to better control them and their causes."

Swan mentioned that the process was inefficient, but could be improved. Making production releases was painful since the process was too slow. Mr. Ride or Die now cut her off:

"How old are you?"

"25 years old."

"Well, your lifespan amounts to the time I have worked for this company, so I guess I have enough experience to decide whether the process is efficient or not. What you are asking for will cause an even bigger problem since it will increase the number of issues and faulty releases, not to mention we would lose tracking of who is responsible for the releases. We won't implement the changes you are asking for. Period."

I left the room shaking, not because of Mr. Ride or Die's refusal, but how he had spoken to Swan. I asked her how she felt, and her answer surprised me: "Fine, it is not the first time this happens to me". How many times have we gone through something like this to the point it becomes normal?

An idea should not be criticized based on the age, gender or level of education of a person. We look for people with different backgrounds and knowledge to tell them what to do, all the while not letting them share their own experiences and creativity. This only keeps us living in a box with the same thoughts. **If we want to do things differently, we must allow others to think differently and put forth their ideas.**

I asked the Chief for his opinion. He said he would escalate the situation with the managing director, but he believed there would be no changes since this might not be considered relevant for Huge Company. In any case, we should know how to choose our battles.

I understand change or different ideas will cause fear and rejection, and this may find you some enemies within an organization or be frowned upon for going against what is customary. It was clear to me that the Chief did not push the envelope because he would rather cover our backs as much as his own. All things considered, Mr. Ride or Die had a lot of time in the company, people listened to him and his proposals and processes were respected.

The "Fix it" team gathered to discuss what had happened. It was not an easy conversation to have. Ed kept saying they were crazy for not listening to our proposal. I empathized, but I thought that they were crazy for doing the same thing over and over, yet demand different results. Eddie asked if it was possible to ask someone from the Production or Rollout department for their help without anybody knowing and work under the radar.

We could, but it would have to be somebody willing to risk their job and accept an extra workload. We all thought about Lucious, who usually helped us with the rollout processes. We bought him a coffee in the cafeteria and told him our proposal. After three cups of coffee, Lucious wanted to know if Mr. Ride or Die was aware about this and how long we would need his help. He told us he had think about it. As I walked back to my place, I kept wondering why we had to raise such a proposal behind everyone's back. What's wrong with wanting to do things differently?

After a few days, the Chief called me and Swan to update us about his meeting with the executive board. It had been brief, and the message was categorical: no any changes would be implemented in the process, and the matter was not to be discussed anymore. Swan and I looked amazed at each other, we could not understand such a strong refusal to a relatively simple change.

I asked the Chief why they rejected the change. Swan added that she did not understand. There were other interests behind the decision and the best was to look for improvement alternatives without modifying the Production department's process or asking for their support: they had certification that endorsed that process and prevented them from changing specifics of it. If they were to keep the certification, the change had to be general. **This bureaucratic mindset is very limiting on analysis and adaptation, but most of all, it hinders the possibility to experiment or make small changes in certain areas that would benefit from it.**

I was so angry I asked no more questions. I simply left the meeting. On our way back, Swan reminded me we were still waiting for Lucious' answer. At that moment I disregarded it, thinking if our leaders were not willing to take risks and experiment, then why should I? **Negative thoughts are easier to accept or imitate since you simply have to be passive,** stay still and let things run their course. Luckily, there are always people around us willing to seek alternatives, like the "Fix it" team in my case.

Ed, Edd and Eddie asked what had happened, and we gave the bad news. The only thing they said was ask about Lucious say. It seemed like he was our only hope. Not wanting to be invasive, we gave him time until he could come to an answer. But we never thought we would get it so soon, nor how we got it.

Lucious asked Swan have a coffee with him. She said she could, but wanted me go as well and discuss our proposal. In fact, he wanted to talk about that, but it was best if I did not go. On her way to the cafeteria, Swan went by my place to say she would be meeting Lucious. An hour later, she sat next to me and told me what Lucious had said.

"Lucious cannot help us. Apparently, after our meeting with Mr. Ride or Die, they met with the Production and Rollout departments and told them that any changes to the established process had to be discussed with management."

Making changes without authorization would be considered serious misconduct since it would invalidate their process certificates. If the teams were audited, there could be warnings and even fines. Furthermore, if they held meetings with the "Fix it" team or any of its members, they should inform management and loop Iveme in. The rationale was the team was trying to change the certified process without the authorization from management, and that was a decision beyond their hierarchy.

I fully understood Lucious and did not want to risk his job. Also, I was amazed at the response we got for being proactive and showing initiative to improve things.

I was devastated. It seemed like the "Fix it" team had turned into public enemy number one. After being the team that brought release incidents to zero, that was constant in its work pace, that fostered collaboration and shared not only our knowledge of codes, but also our way of working, our will to go above and beyond had made us a troublesome team.

One for the road

Wanderer, there is no road, the road is made by walking.
—Antonio Machado

After the limitations to collaborate with the Release and Production departments, we faced problems with our workload. They were asking for greater results from us, but they would not allow us to solve the problems we had identified. Our only solution was extra time.

Wanting to clear my mind and minimize the frustration and helplessness I felt, I went more regularly to the community sessions as a way of asking for help outside of Huge Company. The Viking thought it would be good to share the agility—related work we did. Since we were not big on public speaking, he gave the talk, while we helped with the content.

When our scheduled day came, there were people from many companies. Although I would not deliver the talk, I felt happy for being part of the experience. The presentation lasted fifteen minutes, but there were a lot of questions from the audience which we helped answer, especially when these had a very specific context.

The networking part began, and a former coworker from Huge Company introduced me to his current boss, whom we will call Clooney. He wanted to know about my experience with Kanban, specifically our interactions with other areas, our dependencies and how to manage them. I told him a little about our work with the "Fix it" team. After a few hours, Clooney had to leave, but he gave me his business card to keep on talking.

That had been a very pleasant conversation, but that agreeable sensation ended when I went back to the cruel reality. While the community appreciated us for sharing and looking forward, in the company we were branded as troublesome and slow.

As the leader of my team, I did not want to force them to work extra hours, but we were not meeting the expectations. Furthermore, in our conversations to find solutions, my frustration surfaced in the shape of angry remarks about other areas. BeeGee suggested to hold an improvement session with the executive board, but I lacked the power to request it, and the Chief was not willing to raise the subject again. The Viking, Daysi and Jaime, noticing my frustration, suggested changing positions to a different area. They had heard the Management department needed people. Thus, I had an interview with people from the area; it seemed like a promising opportunity.

On my way back to my desk, I ran into Daysi, and she asked how I was doing in the interviews. I felt like I was doing fine, but still had to talk to the head of Management. She also asked me if I had discussed the possibility of me changing positions with the "Fix it" team. I still had not told them anything, but I would once I knew the change was a fact. Daysi cut me off to tell me that if I really appreciated my team, I had to tell them my intentions so they could decide what to do if that change took effect.

She was right. We had gone through so many things and learned so much together that I could not just leave them without a timely notice. We had a meeting to talk about how we felt and share our ideas for the future.

It is amazing how talking about our vision for the future can make us understand our behavior. They felt the future was uncertain because the lack of collaboration with Mr. Ride or Die was making me react negatively. I was distracted and moody. Swan was concerned about increasing our throughput and stayed extra hours to finish on time the tickets for releases. Ed, Edd and Eddie were at a crossroads because they did not know whether to behave like me or like Swan.

I apologized and told them I was looking to change positions, although I was still going through interviews. I tried to cool the waters by saying that I would only switch areas, but we would still see each other, and that I would push for greater change and improvements in their process from my new position. Changing my place in the hierarchy could even have a positive influence on our project.

At the end of that day, I received an email that would significantly change our plans. It was from Clooney, telling me he had found very interesting our conversation in the event of the community, and he had an open position in a project he was working on. But he needed to hire someone urgently, so I had to go for an interview as soon as possible and make a decision.

I hurried to tell Daysi right then. I wanted a change, but I was scared of doing it elsewhere since I had worked in Huge Company for many years and I did not want to drop all the knowledge I had of our processes. Jaime joined the conversation and asked if I really believed a change of area would make things different. We talked about the comfort zone I was probably in, and my fear of outgrowing it. I even felt like a failure for leaving not only Huge Company, but the entire "Fix it" team just because I did not want to look for ways to prompt change from the inside.

I replied to Clooney accepting the interview. By the end of it, I already had an answer. "We are interested in collaborating with you." **It is incredible how a different vision of our reality and perception can change everything. While in some places I was considered problematic, elsewhere I was an interesting person.**

We began the recruitment process, and we got the paperwork ready to sign the contract. The next day, I told Jaime and Daysi. They were excited and sad at the same time. We had been friends and partners for many years, and now things were ending.

My resignation would be official in two weeks, so HR was working on the paperwork. The news spread like wildfire through Huge Company. I met with the team and told them the news. It was a very emotional conversation, since the last time we had only discussed a change of area. To celebrate and say our goodbyes, we would go to a bar at the end of the day.

Then the Chief called me in. He seemed upset. He was aware about me wanting to change areas and supported me to make that happen, but this decision had rendered that effort useless. He also apologized, since he had to leave for a trip that afternoon, and he would not be able to show up to the bar and bid me farewell. A hug and a handshake was his way of saying: "You'll do just fine." After that party and the two weeks during which I handed in the last of my work, I grabbed my things and took off.

Epilogue

Behind all great human achievements, there is a great team.
—Sergio E. Zamora Rubio

That's right, dear reader. You might recall that, at the beginning of this story, I said I would tell you about the time I "almost" succeeded in becoming an agilist. This story made me feel a bit like a looser because we were unable to adapt, while our interactions with an area we depended on were restricted. However, I firmly believe this was a first step in my journey to becoming an agilist.

I later found out Mr. Ride or Die retired. This meant the change we had proposed would no longer be hindered. It turns out that the whole of the Rollout team was outsourced and their pay depended on the number of tickets they closed. That explained why they would not process more releases with less tickets.

While we saw the possibility of increasing value to our clients (outcomes) by making more changes in less time, the Rollout team saw that their work, or what was used to measure it (output), would diminish, thus reducing their pay. That is a good reason to constantly check and update what we measure, since this has an impact on our behavior. Now that I know this, I think I could have shown more empathy towards the Rollout department and learn about their process and metrics. If this scenario ever happens again, I will probably act differently.

And that is the meaning of being an agilist: constant learning. These were very important moments and experiences. I have fond memories of my coworkers. With some I forged a friendship that still lives on, and I will always be grateful to everyone who was a part of this journey. Today I can say I made the right decision, although I think **there is no such thing as right or wrong choices, only decisions made or not made.** For example, I decided to work and live in Sweden, which inspired me to write this book. I can say this was the right decision when I look up at the sky and see the Northern Lights with my wife.

I want to thank you for getting this far. Below you will find a picture of the board we used in the "Fix it" team.

STOP
PLANNING
AND
START
FINISHING

THE STORY OF AN AGILIST

de Sergio Zamora